Quotes

Of

Justin Bieber

Funny, inspirational & and sometimes strange quotes of Justin Bieber

Terms Of Use Agreement

Every effort had been made to fulfill requirements with regard to reproducing copyrighted material. The author and the publisher will be glad to certify any omissions at the earliest opportunity.

Disclaimer

The author and the publisher have used their best efforts in preparing this book. The author and the publisher make no representation or warranties with respect to the accuracy, fitness, applicability, or completeness of the contents of this work and specifically disclaim all warranties, including without limitation warranties of fitness for a particular purpose. This work is sold with the understanding that author and the publisher is not engaged in rendering legal, or any other professional services.

The information contained in this book is strictly for educational purposes. Therefore, if you wish to apply ideas contained within this book, you are taking full responsibility for your actions. The author and the publisher disclaim any warranties (express or implied), merchantability, or fitness for any particular purpose.

Justin Bieber Quotes

Of course, I think that people are just waiting for that time when I make a mistake and they're gonna jump on it.... There's gonna be haters.
— Justin Bieber

I make mistakes growing up. I'm not perfect; I'm not a robot.
— Justin Bieber

I'm looking forward to influencing others in a positive way. My message is you can do anything if you just put your mind to it.
— Justin Bieber

I'm crazy, I'm nuts. Just the way my brain works. I'm not normal. I think differently.
— Justin Bieber

It's not me trying to act or pose in a certain way. It's a lifestyle - like a suaveness or a swag, per se.
— Justin Bieber

Now that I'm on top, everyone wants to bring me down. Everyone's trying to tug at me and take my spot.
— Justin Bieber

Not trying to be arrogant, but if I walked down the street and a girl saw me, she might take a look back because maybe I'm good-looking, right?
— Justin Bieber

I got a bright future ahead of me.
— Justin Bieber

I leave the hip thrusts to Michael Jackson.
— Justin Bieber

It's cool when fans spend so much time making things for me. It means a lot.
— Justin Bieber

I want my world to be fun.
— Justin Bieber

My manager is definitely a mentor as well as Usher.
— Justin Bieber

I started singing about three years ago, I entered a local singing competition called Stratford Idol. The other people in the competition had been taking singing lessons and had vocal coaches. I wasn't taking it too seriously at the time, I would just sing around the house. I was only 12 and I got second place.

— Justin Bieber

I want to be a young dad. By 25 or 26 I want to see myself, like, married or start looking for a family.

— Justin Bieber

Friends are the best to turn to when you're having a rough day.

— Justin Bieber

I grew up below the poverty line; I didn't have as much as other people did. I think it made me stronger as a person, it built my character. Now I have a 4.0 grade point average and I want to go to college, and just become a better person.

— Justin Bieber

The Beliebers have done some pretty crazy stuff. Last week, the night before I was due to do a show in Germany, four girls went into a dumpster so they could sneak into the building. They climbed in and hid. When the guys working on the truck started getting the garbage they found them straight away. It was crazy.

— Justin Bieber

My mind's always racing.

— Justin Bieber

I know who I am and what I'm doing in my life and what I've accomplished and continue to accomplish as a performer, as a writer, as an artist, as a person, as a human being.

— Justin Bieber

No one can stop me.

— Justin Bieber

Young people in the business have grown up and made the wrong decisions, or bad decisions, and haven't been

good role models. To be someone that people look up to is important to me.
— Justin Bieber

Cheryl Cole and Katy Perry are two of the hottest girls in the world - and so normal and funny with it. If I was a few years older they are the kind of girls I'd like to date. I want a younger version of Cheryl and Katy - a mixture of the two would be hot.
— Justin Bieber

I'm really an animal guy. I express myself in different ways as an animal.
— Justin Bieber

Canada's the best country in the world.
— Justin Bieber

I've never made a bad song.
— Justin Bieber

I've had a few gigs where things have got out of hand and there has been a huge crush with my fans. They

are important and I don't want them being hurt. They are a mad crowd.
— Justin Bieber

I think I'm probably gonna quit music.
— Justin Bieber

I grew up in a really small town with not a lot of money, and I liked singing, but it was just something that was a hobby.
— Justin Bieber

I've got my eye on a few things to spend my money on. I've got my own bank card but I am really good with money. I don't spend too much at all.
— Justin Bieber

A lot of people who are religious, I think they get lost. They go to church just to go to church.
— Justin Bieber

I think older people can appreciate my music because I really show my heart when I sing, and it's not corny. I

think I can grow as an artist, and my fans will grow with me.
— Justin Bieber

As I get into it more, I want to grow as an artist, as an entertainer, and basically perfect my craft.
— Justin Bieber

I want to figure out myself as a man.
— Justin Bieber

I'm happy with the man I'm becoming.
— Justin Bieber

I want to grow as an artist, and I'm taking a step out. I want my music to mature.
— Justin Bieber

When people see a negative thing about me on a magazine, they're gonna buy it. Every time some site writes something bad, all my followers go on there, and it brings them more traffic.
— Justin Bieber

Sometimes it's overwhelming but I love my fans and it's always great to see them.
— Justin Bieber

We're trying to set up a movie for me in the near future. It's going to be similar to the story of how I got discovered. Kinda like my own version of '8 Mile.'
— Justin Bieber

"I'm telling you, people. Everyday we wake up is another blessing. Follow your dreams and don't let anyone stop you. Never say never."
— Justin Bieber

"Two people can look at the same thing and see it differently.."
— Justin Bieber

"Never say never"
— Justin Bieber

"A girl has to have a beautiful smile, Beautiful eyes and she should have a good sense of humor.

She should be honest, loving and trustworthy."
— Justin Bieber

"Haters will say what they want, but their hate will never stop you from chasing your dream"
— Justin Bieber

"I want my world to be fun. No parents, no rules, no nothing. Like, no one can stop me. No one can stop me."
— Justin Bieber

"I'm just a regular 16 year old kid. I make good grilled cheese and I like girls."
— Justin Bieber

"There's gonna be times when people tell you that you can't live your dreams, this is what I tell them, Never Say Never."
— Justin Bieber

"Born to be somebody." You were born to be somebody, maybe a vet, maybe a hero, maybe a caregiver.

Whatever it is you were born to be something special
and if you believe you can achieve"
— Justin Bieber

"Someone once told me to never dream.
I said NEVER SAY NEVER"
— Justin Bieber

"If i can do just one tenth of the good
Michael Jackson did for others, i can really make a
difference in this world"
— Justin Bieber, First Step 2 Forever

"My world got very big,
very fast, and based on a lot of sad examples
from the past,
a lot of people expect me to get lost in it"
— Justin Bieber

"The success I've achieved comes to me from God"
— Justin Bieber, Justin Bieber: My World

"I'm not a fighter by nature, but, if I believe in something, I stand up for it"
— Justin Bieber

"I'm looking forward to influencing others in a positive way. My message is you can do anything if you just put your mind to it."
— Justin Bieber

"I think older people can appreciate my music because I really show my heart when I sing, and it's not corny. I think I can grow as an artist, and my fans will grow with me."
— Justin Bieber

"Keep Going Strong!"
— Justin Bieber

"I grew up below the poverty line; I didn't have as much as other people did. I think it made me stronger as a person, it built my character. Now I have a 4.0 grade point average and I want to go to college, and just become a better person."
— Justin Bieber

"I wrote the song 'Down to Earth' a few years ago, and i was really excited to record it for My World album. It's a huge fan favourite. So many people feel where i'm coming from. It doesn't need any spectacular stage effects in the touring show; the best thing i can do is just sing it straight from my heart. I'm not afraid to show my emotions; if you love someone, you should tell them. If you think a girl is beautiful, you should say that. Usher says some songs work best when there's a sob in the singer's voice. You gotta let that deep feeling come through. And that's how i felt about this song. Sometimes the emotion of it is enough to bring tears to my eyes."
— Justin Bieber

"Every one of my fans is so special to me"
— Justin Bieber

"Never Say Never if you know you can do what you love don't give up."
— Justin Bieber

"You know me...I can't resist a good prank"
— Justin Bieber, First Step 2 Forever

"Pranks vs school = pranks win all day"
— Justin Bieber

"Never say never see what is possible if you never give up"
— Justin Bieber

"I will never say never i will fight i will fight till forever make it right whenever you knock me down i will not stay on the ground pick it up and never say never"
— Justin Bieber

"Whenever I'm sick, my doctor jokes that I have Bieber Fever!"
— Justin Bieber

"I liked this girl in my sixth grade class. I dared her to kiss me -- but she didn't!"
— Justin Bieber

"Sometimes people say that you can not live your dreams. Sometimes people say that you can not sell out

madison square garden. Well this is what i tell them -
NEVER SAY NEVER"
— Justin Bieber

"There's gonna be times in life when people tell you that
you can't, thats when you just gotta turn around and
say watch me."
— Justin Bieber

"No matter how much I try, I can't figure out how to not
be adorable!"
— Justin Bieber

"So many people will tell you that you can't but all you
gotta do is turn around and say "Watch me"
— Justin Bieber

"No matter how talented you are not everyone is going
to like you but that's life, stay strong"
— Justin Bieber

"You can't always get what you want. But, if you're
lucky, you get what you need."
— Justin Bieber

"So remember this is a bieber world. You're just living in it. Bieber or die."
— Justin Bieber

"You should not be afraid of doing what ur mind tells you 2 do...just listen 2 ur heart...never say never"
— Justin Bieber

"What makes the perfect kiss? Closing your eyes when you kiss is important. Or lifting up the leg, but that's more of a girl thing, I'm manly. Passion is good! She brings out the best in me. (Selena)"
— Justin Bieber

"It's a Bieber world live it or die."
— Justin Bieber

"I don't like it when a girl trys to hard and puts loads of makeup on. You gotta show some of yourself."
— Justin Bieber

"Chicken is good and never stop eating you will look like

me and you will have hair like me and sing like me and be 500 pounds!!!!"
— Justin Bieber

"Everything starts from something but something would be nothing if your heart didn't dream with me."
— Justin Bieber

"God speaks in the silence of the heart
Listening is the beginning of prayer."
— Justin Bieber

"I won't even pretend I didn't care. I wanted to win. I mean, if you don't care about winning the competition, why show up?"
— Justin Bieber

"If you don't dream big, there's no use of dreaming. If you don't have faith, there's nothing worth believing."
— Justin Bieber

"We didn't have time to go tobogganing, because we didn't have the toboggan."
— Justin Bieber

"Why do u drive on a parkway and park in the driveway. It's messed up."
— Justin Bieber

"This letter really touched my heart. Sabrina says when she lost all her hair during chemo, she wore the cap I gave her."
— Justin Bieber

"When Chuck Norris stands in front of a mirror it shatters because the mirror knows never to stand between CHUCK NORRIS and CHUCK NORRIS."
— Justin Bieber

"When we got to the marina we saw this beautiful boat named Tara waiting for us. Fredo, Carin, Ryan, Dan, Kenny, Allison, my mom, and me were all together to enjoy that extraordinary day. As the boat pulled away from the city, its skyline vanished into the horizon. The captain took us to this area where we sailed through caves and lush hilly landscapes. All of a sudden, the captain pushed the throttle all the way down and we started bombing across the water like we were in a James Bond movie. Everyone's hair was blowing all over

the place, especially the girls'. Of course, mine was perfect (ha,ha), but theirs ended up looking like the worst case of bedhead I've seen! It was so funny."
— Justin Bieber

"We never destroyed anything major, but there were a few small casualties. A couple of lamps were sacrificed."
— Justin Bieber

"I want you here with me To guide me, hold me, and love me now"
— Justin Bieber

"I just want to be young and fun and you know I think people should all wear yellow shoes."
— Justin Bieber

"Music is the universal language no matter the country we are born in or the color of our skin. Bring us all together"
— Justin Bieber

"When life pushes you down on your knees you're in the perfect position to pray"
— Justin Bieber

"Flowers are nice, but love is better."
— Justin Bieber

"But the grass ain't always greener on the other side, It's green where you water it"
— Justin Bieber

"There's gonna be times in your life when people say you can't do something. And there's gonna be times in your life when people say that you can't live your dreams. This is what I tell them: Never say never!"
— Justin Bieber

"I still feel like a regular kid. Sometimes it's weird that i go to places and have thousands of people waiting for me. But i always think, I'm Justin..."
— Justin Bieber

"When I hear him sing and see what he can do, though, it's always a reminder of why I look up to Usher as my

mentor and why I will always be an Usher fan to my core. But I'm lucky to say that he's an even better friend to me than he's a mentor. He's truly the real deal."
— Justin Bieber

"I'm living proof that dreams do come true. Work hard. Pray. Believe."
— Justin Bieber

"Don't sweat, don't cry, we don't need no wings to fly."
— Justin Bieber

"I have the most incredible fans in the world- and I'm grateful for each and every one."
— Justin Bieber

" I'm here to bless not to impress"
— Justin Bieber

"You see, my buddies had a freedom I no longer had. All I wanted was to do something normal and skateboard with the guys, but i knew that if I went

downstairs to join them it would create total chaos."
— Justin Bieber

"In life u will make mistakes and people will try and tear u down...but u gotta stay positive. Stay strong..and learn to be better..and..always live to serve others and The Lord."

"Haters are just confused admirers"
— Justin Bieber

"Before this amazing journey began i'd never set foot outside of Canada. Now I've traveled the world and seen so many amazing things. In that sense, my story is something I like to share with others to show that anything is possible."
— Justin Bieber

"You don't need to go to church to be a Christian. If you go to Taco Bell, that doesn't make you a taco."
— Justin Bieber

"When you've reached a certain point in your life, there are people out there waiting to see you fall. but rather

than let gravity take you down, sometimes you have to take matters into your own hands and fly."
— Justin Bieber

"I have crushes, but they're all too old. Like Beyonce - she has a husband, I might get shot. I went up to give Beyonce a hug at the Grammy's and Jay-Z said, watch out buddy! He was kidding, but you know..."
— Justin Bieber

"I'm telling you, people. Everyday we wake up is another blessing. Follow your dreams and don't let anyone stop you. Never say never."
— Justin Bieber

I know my friends, family and fans know the person I am. Hearing adults spread lies and rumors is part of their job I guess. But all I have to say is... kill them with kindness.
— Justin Bieber

"I'm a really claustrophobic person to begin with. I hate elevators, especially cramped elevators. I get really scared. So I think that it's very definitely scary when

girls are all around me and I can't go anywhere. At the same time, I guess I got to get used to it, you know what I mean?"
— Justin Bieber

"My mom said I wasn't allowed to date until I was sixteen, but I broke that rule. She found out and said, 'I'm disappointed in you.'
— Justin Bieber

"I really don't believe in abortion. It's like killing a baby?"
— Justin Bieber

"I have dumped a girl over the phone – it's terrible isn't it? We got into an argument during a phone call so I basically said, I don't wanna be with you any more,' and she cried. I saw her after that and it was a bit awkward, but we're not enemies now, so that's cool. But I wouldn't recommend it, it's very mean!"
— Justin Bieber

"It would be a shame to go out with a hot girl you can't have a decent conversation with!"
— Justin Bieber

"To all the haters out there I wish u the best. U cant bring me down. I wake up everyday grateful 4 the opportunity and grateful to the fans."
— Justin Bieber

"It was like, Usher and Timberlake want to meet me? Are you kidding? There was no point in trying to tell anyone at school about this. It would be like telling them I was going to meet CHUCK NORRIS, and we all know that guy is untouchable. I mean, c'mon. It's CHUCK NORRIS. He doesn't need Twitter, he's already following you."
— Justin Bieber

"I also try to read all of my fan mail. A lot of them send me candy, which I'm not allowed to eat 'cause my mom says it might be poisonous."
— Justin Bieber

"It's kind of hard to balance school and work sometimes. But sometimes, like, if I'm going to the White House and I'm in there doing a tour and stuff, that's like school."
— Justin Bieber

"It's funny when I read things about myself that r just not true. Why would certain people take time out of their day to hate on a 16 yr old?"
— Justin Bieber

"Singers aren't supposed to have dairy before a show, but we all know I'm a rule breaker. Pizza is just so good!
— Justin Bieber

"I think she's cute. And, no, she's not too old for me. Above 40 is a little too old for me." on Kim Kardashian
— Justin Bieber

"My first date has been sort of mythologized as 'Bieber's Dating Disaster.' I took her to King's a buffet restaurant. Yes, I wore a white shirt. Yes, I got spaghetti."

— Justin Bieber

"There are lots of things I really like besides girls. Like pizza. And pranking. And CHUCK NORRIS."

— Justin Bieber

"It was like I opened my eyes one day and noticed that the world was full of beautiful girls. And I've had a hard time hard time thinking about anything else since then."

— Justin Bieber

"Two people can look at the same thing and see it differently.."

— Justin Bieber

"I want my world to be fun. No parents, no rules, no nothing. Like, no one can stop me. No one can stop me."

— Justin Bieber

"My world got very big, very fast, and based on a lot of
sad examples from the past, a lot of people expect me
to get lost in it"
— Justin Bieber

"If I notice a cute girl at the meet-and-greet, I might go
and talk to her."
— Justin Bieber

"I think older people can appreciate my music because I
really show my heart when I sing, and it's not corny. I
think I can grow as an artist, and my fans will grow with
me."
— Justin Bieber

"Haters will say what they want, but their hate will
never stop you from chasing your dream"
— Justin Bieber

"I want girls to hear my music and want to play it again
because it made their hearts feel good."
— Justin Bieber

"I always thank God for giving me this opportunity and for blessing me with this talent."
— Justin Bieber

"I love that my fans are so devoted, because without them i wouldn't have this opportunity."
— Justin Bieber

"My fans will grow up with me."
— Justin Bieber

"We only live once so follow your dreams and never say never!"
— Justin Bieber

"I take it with a grain of salt. It's been incredible, my fans are amazing and I wouldn't have it any other way "
— Justin Bieber

"The blessing is not about being able to receive as much as it is being in a position to give back to others."
— Justin Bieber

"Now that I'm on top, everyone wants to bring me down. Everyone's trying to tug at me and take my spot."
— Justin Bieber

"I give up a personal life... to pursue what I love and make my fans happy."
— Justin Bieber

"You know, there's a lot of people that look up to me and i'm not always gonna be perfect .. I make bad decision sometimes."
— Justin Bieber